# BENJAMIN LEES

# PIANO TRIO No. 2

## "Silent Voices"

BOOSEY & HAWKES

DISTRIBUTED BY

HAL•LEONARD®
CORPORATION

7777 W. BLUEMOUND RD. P.O. BOX 13819 MILWAUKEE, WI 53213

www.boosey.com
www.halleonard.com

Commissioned by Steven Honigberg and the United States Holocaust Memorial Museum

First performed 31 May, 1998 at the
United States Holocaust Memorial Museum,
Washington, DC
by George Marsh, violin
Steven Honigberg, violoncello
Joseph Holt, piano


Recorded by the same performers
on Albany Records Troy 518

COMPOSER'S NOTE

This work represents a small gesture of remembrance to those whose voices were forever stilled by pogroms and genocides of the past. I have tried to blend the elements of drama, grief and lyricism into a very compact musical statement in the hope that this will be communicated to the audience.

The work is in one movement but comprises several sections. From the very outset there is an extended statement by the violin accompanied by the cello. Next, the cello picks up the statement while the violin assumes the counter voice. Finally, the piano enters with the same statement, this time accompanied by the violin and cello. From that point on, there are some developments of this idea before subsequent sections make their appearance. The final section is quite dramatic, slowly dying away into silence. The work is a contrast between stark drama and poignant lyricism.

*—Benjamin Lees*

Duration: *ca.* 14 minutes

# PIANO TRIO No 2
## "Silent Voices"

BENJAMIN LEES
1998

M-051-10610-3

2

4

# PIANO TRIO No 2
## "Silent Voices"

**Violin**

BENJAMIN LEES
1998

M-051-10610-3

Violin

**Violoncello**

# PIANO TRIO No 2
## "Silent Voices"

BENJAMIN LEES
1998

4

Violoncello

15

M-051-10610-3

21

M-051-10610-3

February 17, 1998
Palm Springs, California